CHATSWORTH AND THE VISITOR

Chatsworth has been open for people to see round ever since it was built. Travellers who wrote about it in the 17th and early 18th centuries include Celia Fiennes and Daniel Defoe. In 1775 an inn (now the estate office and club) was built at Edensor for the convenience of the sightseers.

In the 18th century the family lived mostly in London, but the housekeeper had instructions to show people round, and when the Fifth Duke and Georgiana were here there were 'open days' when dinner was even provided.

When the 6th Duke (1790-1858) was making his alterations and additions, including the Great Conservatory, the house and garden attracted much attention. The following extract from *The Mirror of Literature and Amusement* of February 1844 shows that all were welcome at Chatsworth:

"The Duke of Devonshire allows all persons whatsoever to see the mansion and grounds every day in the year, Sundays not excepted, from 10 in the morning till 5 in the afternoon. The humblest individual is not only shown the whole, but the Duke has expressly ordered the waterworks to be played for everyone without exception. This is acting in the true spirit of great wealth and enlightened liberality; let us add, also, in the spirit of wisdom."

In 1849 the Midland Railway from Derby reached Rowsley, three miles down the Derwent valley, and 80,000 people came to see the house during the summer. No charge was made until the 9th Duke succeeded in 1908, when the resulting income was given to local hospitals. During the last war the house was occupied by a girls' boarding school, Penrhos College. 300 pupils and teachers lived and worked here

Chatsworth has grown over the years into what you see today. Only the Chapel and the State Dining Room (1690s), the Great Dining Room and the Sculpture Gallery (1830s), are virtually unaltered since they were built. So it is with the contents. No room is a set piece of furniture of the date of the building. Pictures and furniture from other houses have arrived at Chatsworth and have settled where they look most suitable. Nor is the Collection a static one, and a visitor to the house need not always expect to see the same things on two different visits. New acquisitions are added, many by the present Duke; paintings are lent to exhibitions for long periods, and ideas on arrangement and decoration constantly change. As long as Chatsworth remains a family home this is how it will be.

from 1939–1946. The State Rooms and corridors became dormitories and the drawing rooms and larger bedrooms were class rooms. The furniture and pictures were stored in the Library and Sculpture Gallery.

After the war the house was gradually prepared for re-opening to the public. The 10th Duke lived in Churchdale Hall, near Ashford-in-the-Water, and in London, and Chatsworth was occupied by a skeleton staff. No decoration was done at that time. Shabby but clean, it was re-opened to the public in 1949 and, in spite of petrol rationing, 75,000 people came round that year. The charge for adults was half-a-crown, and one shilling for the garden. For the first time the proceeds went towards the upkeep and since then the entrance money paid by visitors has made a vital contribution to the maintenance of the house and garden.

A view of Chatsworth from the west
1770, by William Marlow (1740–1813)

Designed and published by Derbyshire Countryside Ltd., Derby DE1 3HE. Tel: (01332) 347087 and printed in Great Britain.

Text by The Duchess of Devonshire.

Photography mainly by Peter Smith AMPA., ABIPP., of Newbery Smith Photography, with additional photographs by Ian Fraser-Martin. Front cover photograph by Mike Williams. Painting of the State Rooms by Nick McCann.

ISBN 0 85100 118 1

Chatsworth in 1828 from a watercolour
by William Cowen (1797–1861)

Opposite:
The North Entrance

THE APPROACH

The approach to the house is under the arch of the Porter's Lodge between an avenue of tulip trees (*Liriodendron tulipifera*), with the long wing, added 1820–27, on your left. This massive building including the high tower, or *belvedere*, above the Theatre at the north end was built for the 6th, 'Bachelor' Duke (1790–1858) by Sir Jeffry Wyatville (1766–1840).

It contains the offices, old kitchens, laundry, servants' hall, lamp room, still room, boiler room, carpenter's shop, many bedrooms, the Great Dining Room, Sculpture Gallery, Orangery and Theatre.

The weeping ash by the front door was brought from a Derby garden in 1830 when it was already over 40 years old.

Queen Victoria arriving at Chatsworth 1843

THE NORTH FRONT HALL

The North Front Hall was the kitchen until the 1760s and the kitchen ranges still exist behind the fireplaces. *Bolton Abbey in the Olden Time* by Sir Edwin Landseer (1802–73) hangs on the right hand wall as you enter. The 6th Duke's Russian coachman posed for the keeper kneeling beside the stag. The marble mother and child, and the full-length figure of a man are Roman, 1st century A.D. They were found at Apt in Provence and bought by the 6th Duke, who was a passionate collector of statuary. The ceiling painting is after the *Aurora* by Guido Reni.

One of two Hall Porter's chairs, early 19th century

Bolton Abbey in the Olden Time
by Sir Edwin Landseer (1802–73)

Bolton Abbey is part of the Yorkshire estate
of the Duke of Devonshire

6

Balsa wood model of
Chatsworth by J. A. Dent,
1977–79. Scale 1:200

THE NORTH CORRIDOR

Part of the coloured marble pavement, 1841, "by Leonardi, a poor man who lives at the Forum in Rome"

This passage was originally an open colonnade through which visitors entering by the West Front (the entrance until the 1760s) had to pass before arriving in the Painted Hall, and very cold it must have been. The 6th Duke enclosed it and in 1841 the coloured marble pavement was laid to divert the eye from the irregularities of the architecture. When it was first put down "so brightly was it polished it was difficult to make anybody walk on it," he wrote. The mahogany chairs and settees were designed by William Kent (1685–1748) for Chiswick Villa and Devonshire House, two London houses which belonged to the family. On the walls are small paintings by lesser masters of the 17th century. The tall portrait on an easel is of Andrew Cavendish, 11th Duke of Devonshire, and was painted by Stephen Conroy (b. 1953) in 1992–3.

Hall chair, mahogany, designed by William Kent (1685–1748)

THE PAINTED HALL

The upper part of the hall has not been changed since it was painted in 1692–4 with scenes from the life of Julius Caesar by Louis Laguerre (1663–1721), but the ground floor and stairs have been altered several times. The marble floor replaced stone in 1779 and was relaid by the 6th Duke in 1834. He inserted three French windows into the courtyard in the 1820s. Before that there was a painted wainscot along the west wall and it must have been very dark. The staircase has been altered twice since the 1st Duke's twin curved stairs were built.

The architect Sir Jeffry Wyatville (1766–1840) designed a single flight and matching galleries along the east and west walls in 1833. They were demolished and replaced by the present stairs and single gallery, designed by W.H. Romaine-Walker for the 9th Duke of Devonshire in 1912. The gilt ironwork was copied from the balustrade wrought (1689) by the French smith Jean Tijou on the Great Stairs above, leading to the second floor.

Three of the four flower paintings are probably by Jean-Baptiste Monnoyer (1636–99), the fourth is signed by Jakob Bogdany (1660–1724).

Over the fireplace the 6th Duke's Latin inscription, translated, reads 'William Spencer Duke of Devonshire inherited this most beautiful house from his father in the year 1811, which had been begun in the year of English liberty 1688, and completed in the year of his bereavement 1840'. The bereavement refers to the early death of his beloved niece Blanche, Countess of Burlington, the wife of his heir.

The Staircase in the Painted Hall, 1827, watercolour by William Henry Hunt, (1790–1864) showing the original twin curved stairs built for the 1st Duke

Detail of
the painted ceiling

The Painted Hall

Wrought iron balcony on the west wall of the
courtyard, after Jean Tijou (*fl.* 1689–1712)

In 1936 there was nearly a disaster here. The ceiling was
discovered to be sagging and on the point of collapsing onto
the floor 29 feet below. It took two years to make it safe
and during the summers the visitors had to make their way
through a forest of scaffolding. In 1996 the ceiling painting
was restored by Pauline Plummer and her team.

Charitable functions and the children's Christmas party,
a tradition since the 1890s, are held in the Painted Hall.

Opposite:
The Painted Hall looking south

Fountain in the Courtyard

10

THE GREAT STAIRS

An attendant of Neptune on a dolphin. Detail from a neoclassical white marble bath, Italian, early 19th century

On the first floor landing stand two baby carriages and a child's sleigh. One is made to be pulled by a goat and the shafts are in the form of snakes, the family crest. It was probably designed by William Kent for the 3rd Duke's children.

The grey marble basin (1694) under the window was where the dishes from the nearby dining room were rinsed. The white marble bath is l9th century in the classical style. The bronze figure of Mercury was cast for the 6th Duke after the original in Florence by Giambologna.

Door-case carved from Staffordshire alabaster

Several attempts at decoration on the upper walls were made for the 1st Duke. High up are coloured paintings in the style of Verrio's ceiling. There are three sculpted figures by Caius Gabriel Cibber (1630–1700) brought in from the garden in 1692 and busts were placed in the niches. Finding these not enough the Duke had the *grisaille* panels painted on the walls to resemble sculpture. The door-cases are carved in alabaster from Staffordshire.

Opposite:
Bronze statue of *Mercury* after
Giambologna (1529–1608)

Two baby carriages, 18th century, and a child's sleigh, 19th century

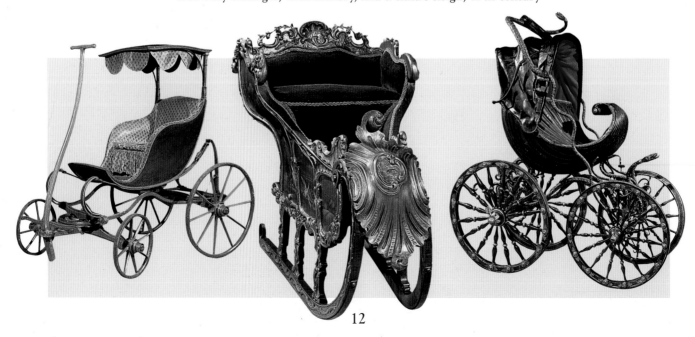

THE STATE ROOMS

State Dressing Room   State Bedroom   State Music Room   State Drawing Room   State Dining Room

These are the grandest rooms of the 1st Duke's building, and took the place of what was the Long Gallery in the Elizabethan house, which explains their unusual position here on the top floor. They were designed for display rather than for living in and the carved woodwork and painted ceilings make a rich background for furniture and pictures. Apartments of state were intended principally for the reception of the King and Queen, but it was not until the reign of Victoria that a monarch visited Chatsworth. So well built is this part of the house you can sit in the family's rooms below and be unaware that there is a crowd of visitors above.

The 6th Duke, in his *Handbook* of 1844, says of the State Dining Room 'It was never dined in that I know of – the first room of this great unappropriated apartment, which consumes in useless display the best habitable part of the house. What bedrooms might have been here with the south sun, and beautiful views! I was much tempted but finished conservatively by repairing the sinking floors and threatening ceilings and as a museum of old furniture and a walk in bad weather I am well contented to retain this dismal, ponderous range of Hampton Court-like chambers'. The State Rooms were dormitories when the house was occupied from 1939–46 by a girls' school, Penrhos College, during the war.

Some people think there is not enough light in these rooms but it is essential sunlight does not reach the furniture, tapestries, pictures and leather-covered walls, as it would soon destroy them.

THE STATE DINING ROOM

The largest of the second floor State Rooms, and unchanged since the 1st Duke's time when it was called 'The Great Chamber'. The ceiling was painted in 1691–2 by Verrio (1639–1707), and was restored 1988–90 by Pauline Plummer and her team. One of the three Fates, *Atropos* (right of the fireplace) cutting the thread of life with her 'abhorred shears' is a portrait of Mrs. Hackett, the 1st Duke's housekeeper, whom Verrio disliked. The mirror in line with the communicating doors, and the same size, was made to double the apparent length of these rooms as seen reflected from the far end.

The gilt side tables were designed by William Kent, probably for Lord Burlington, father-in-law of the 4th Duke. The fish, game-birds, fruit, flowers, foliage and draperies were carved (1692–4) by Samuel Watson, and by Lobb, Young and Davis, the team of carvers from London engaged by the 1st Duke. The window frames of this and the succeeding State Rooms were made in 1954 to match the originals which survive on the West Front, replacing plate glass ordered by the 6th Duke in 1826. The panes have bevelled edges and the frames are of oak from the park.

The pastel portrait by George Knapton (1698–1778) is of Charlotte Boyle, Lord Burlington's daughter and heiress, who married the Marquess of Hartington, later 4th Duke of Devonshire

Detail of Verrio's portrait of
Mrs Hackett

The State Dining Room

Oval portrait, in the carved overmantel,
after Daniel Mytens (*c.* 1590–before 1648),
of *William Clifford 5th Earl of Cumberland*

Portrait of a Little Girl by Cornelis de Vos
(1585–1651) detail left, was bought by the
3rd Earl of Burlington and may be a portrait
of one of the artist's daughters

THE
STATE DRAWING ROOM

Chatsworth in Wartime, 1939, by Edward Halliday (1902–84)

When war broke out in 1939 the buildings of Penrhos College, a girls' school in North Wales,
were taken over by the Ministry of Food and the school moved to Chatsworth.
The Painted Hall was used for assemblies and prayers, the Orangery became the art room,
physics was done in the butler's pantry, biology in the still-room and chemistry,
for safety's sake, in the stables. Dormitories were scattered throughout the house.
Up to 20 girls slept in the State Drawing Room, shown in the painting.
The school left Chatsworth in 1946

The tapestries were woven at Mortlake *c.* 1635 after cartoons of biblical scenes by Raphael (1483–1520), now in the Victoria and Albert Museum. They were probably part of the original decoration of the room, but they have lost their borders and have been cut to fit the available space. The 6th Duke replaced the mouldings round them *c.* 1830.

The ceiling, *c.* 1690, is by Laguerre, *An Assembly of the Gods*, with *The Forge of Vulcan*, and *Vulcan discovering Mars and*

Coromandel lacquer cabinet,
c. 1700

Venus in the covings. The portrait over the fireplace is of the 1st Duke of Devonshire after William Wissing (1656–87). The writing table, chair and side-table, *c.* 1780, are signed by David Roentgen (1743–1807) and the coffers and cabinet are made of coromandel lacquer. The chairs and settees are part of a large set made about 1720 occurring throughout the house covered in different materials. In the 1920s when the 9th Duke's daughters were growing up, a jazz band played here.

An Assembly of the Gods – ceiling painting, *c.* 1690, in the
State Drawing Room by Louis Laguerre (1663–1721)

The Charge to St. Peter. One of the Mortlake tapestry panels, *c.* 1635, woven after Raphael's
cartoons of scenes from the Acts of the Apostles

THE
STATE MUSIC ROOM

The painting of a violin on the inner door is a *trompe l'oeil* (deceives the eye). Even if you are close to it, it is difficult not to touch it to discover if it is real. It was painted by Jan van der Vaart (c. 1653–1727) on a door brought in the 18th century from Devonshire House in Piccadilly (demolished 1924) and installed in this room in 1836. For over 150 years the violin has been one of the best remembered things at Chatsworth.

The stamped and gilded leather (*cuir repoussé*) wall hangings were ordered by the 6th Duke c. 1830 after he saw some at Fontainebleau. There are nine portraits in leather of

him around the frieze. The carved and gilded chairs were used by King George III and Queen Charlotte at their coronation in 1761 and were a perquisite of the 4th Duke as Lord Chamberlain. The green Russian malachite table, clock and urns were given to the 6th Duke by Czar Nicholas I. The two-manual harpsichord was made by Shudi and Broadwood in 1782 and is in excellent playing condition. The four pedestals are by André-Charles Boulle (1642–1732), inlaid with tortoiseshell, pewter and brass. The carpet is English, with a hand-knotted pile, of the late 18th century.

Portrait of the 2nd Duke as a young man attributed to Mary Beale (1633–99)

Right of the fireplace, the *Family Group* is by Paris Bordone (1500–71) and next to this is the large *Blind Belisarius Receiving Alms* bought by the 3rd Earl of Burlington as a Van Dyck, but now attributed to Luciano Borzone (1590–1645). Lord Burlington also bought the other large painting, *Acis and Galatea* by Luca Giordano (1632–1705), and on the next wall hangs *The Procession of the Dogaressa Grimani* by Andrea Vicentino (c. 1539–1614).

The ceiling, c. 1690, is by Laguerre and shows Phaeton begging Apollo to allow him to drive his chariot. The ensuing catastrophe is shown on the coving of the east wall.

One of two coronation thrones of King George III and Queen Charlotte, carved and gilded by Katherine Naish and upholstered by Vile and Cobb, 1761

The State Music Room

The Procession of the Dogaressa Grimani by Andrea Vicentino (c. 1539–1614)

A pedestal by André Charles Boulle (1642–1732) inlaid with tortoiseshell, pewter and brass

Mahogany and satinwood harpsichord by Burkat Shudi and his son-in-law John Broadwood 1782

Russian malachite table and clock presented to the 6th Duke by Czar Nicholas I

THE STATE BEDROOM

The bed belonging to King George II and in which he died was another of the 4th Duke's perquisites as Lord Chamberlain. The original State Bed ordered by the 1st Duke for this room was made by Francis Lapiere in 1697 at the enormous cost of £470, then the most expensive piece of furniture in the house. Its canopy survives at Hardwick Hall. The two large mirrors decorated with the arms of the 1st Duke and Duchess were made in 1703 by John Gumley (*fl.* 1694–1729) and cost £100 each.

The State Bedroom

The stamped and gilded leather is repeated in this room and the ceiling, c. 1690, is by Laguerre, restored and cleaned by the Gibbons brothers in 1973. The subject here is Aurora (Dawn) chasing away Diana (Night). The painted shadows in the covings appear to be cast by light from the windows.

The cabinets are by Boulle and the writing table is in the same style. Boulle furniture, which is a feature of the State Rooms, usually has ormolu mounts and a surface of brass elaborately pierced and inlaid with tortoiseshell. The bedside tables were found by Evelyn Duchess of Devonshire (1870–1960) in a postillion's room over the stables. The fireback is a 1912 fake.

King George V and Queen Mary slept in this bedroom when they stayed at Chatsworth for the Royal Show at Derby in 1933. It was also used by members of the family at Christmas until the Second World War.

Venus and Adonis by
Simon Vouet (1590–1649)

Detail of
Laguerre's ceiling painting

Above:
Europa and the Bull
by Sir Peter Lely
(1618–80)

The silver chandelier, English, is unmarked, but was probably made to celebrate the creation of the Dukedom in 1694. The smaller cherubs each hold a shield with the Cavendish cypher surmounted by an Earl's coronet, but the large one at the top has the coronet of a Duke

Famille verte dish
K'ang Hsi period
(1662–1722)

THE STATE DRESSING ROOM

This is the only room in the house which looks both south and west. The English chandelier is one of the few surviving pieces of silver furniture in this country. The fireplace was added in 1912, based on one at Hampton Court. The ceiling, *c.* 1690, again by Laguerre, shows Juno, Venus and Minerva sending Mercury in search of Paris.

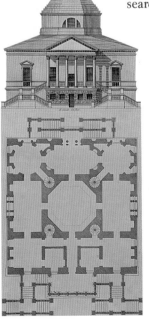

Through the window you can see the pattern of box hedges in the West Garden (private) which is taken from the architectural plan of Chiswick Villa, Lord Burlington's little palace to the west of London. It was planted in 1960. The round pond represents the dome. The plan is one foot out of scale.

THE CHINA CLOSET

In 1995 this room was rehung with green silk damask and fitted with wall-cases to display a porcelain dinner service of more than 200 pieces, made at Berlin *c.* 1780. Each piece, including the handles of the knives and forks, is white porcelain painted with birds perched on branches, butterflies and moths.

The service was originally twice its present size and belonged to Warren Hastings (1732–1818), Governor-General of India. In 1788 Hastings was impeached by the government on grounds of corruption and his trial lasted seven years. Although he was acquitted he was forced to sell much of the contents of his house to pay his costs. Half of the dinner service was bought by his neighbour, John 1st Baron Redesdale, from whom it descended to the father of the present Duchess of Devonshire. When Lord Redesdale sold it in 1948 the Duchess persuaded the present Duke to buy it, as she had always been fascinated by the insects painted on faults in the porcelain on the underside of the plates.

The first Berlin porcelain factory was founded in 1752 and was joined by a second in 1761. They were purchased in 1763 by Frederick the Great of Prussia and Berlin porcelain then entered its most famous period. The factories have continued as a royal and later state-owned concern until the present day.

A detail showing a goldfinch and a mistle thrush

A display of cutlery from the porcelain dinner service *c.* 1780

The South
Sketch Gallery

THE SKETCH
GALLERIES

These passages were added in 1834–5. Till then
you had to walk from room to room. The
collection of Old Master Drawings was hung here till
they were found to be fading and were returned to
their folios. Now portraits of all the dukes are in
these galleries.

The Mortlake tapestries, showing hunting scenes,
are late 17th century. The blue and white tulip vases,
made at Delft in the 1690s, were bought by the 1st
Duke. The separate tiers were filled with water and
each nozzle held a single flower.

Delft tulip vase
by Adriaen Koeks
(active 1687–1701)

28

Some 20th century Family Portraits from the Sketch Galleries

The Duchess of Devonshire
b. 1920
by Pietro Annigoni
(1910–88)

Andrew 11th Duke of Devonshire
b. 1920
by Theodore Ramos
(b. 1920)

William Marquess of Hartington
1917–44
by Sir Oswald Birley
(1880–1952)

Kathleen Kennedy
Marchioness of Hartington
1920–48

Mary Duchess of Devonshire
1895–1988
by Sir James Shannon
(1862–1923)

Evelyn Duchess of Devonshire
1870–1960
by John Singer Sargent
(1856–1925)

Walnut longcase clock
by Thomas Tompion
(1638–1713)

THE WEST STAIRS

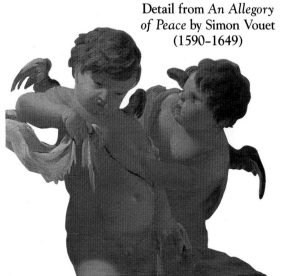

Looking down the West Stairs

A bronze copy of *The Warwick Vase* at the foot of the stairs

the local smith John Gardom in 1702. The ceiling, *The Fall of Phaeton*, was one of the earliest efforts of Sir James Thornhill (1676–1734). The sculpted heads of Sir Roy Strong, HRH The Prince of Wales, Patrick Leigh-Fermor, Harold Macmillan, Lucian Freud, Sir John Betjeman, the present (11th) Duke of Devonshire, his son the Marquess of Hartington and a self-portrait are by Angela Conner, commissioned by the Duke between 1971 and 1995.

At the top of the stairs is *The English Club-House at Florence* by Thomas Patch (1725–82). The painting over the door on the first floor is *An Allegory of Peace* by Simon Vouet (1590–1649), which was probably painted for Anne of Austria, Queen of Louis XIII of France. Her arms appear on the shield to the right. The carved stone tablet showing the names and dates of the Dukes of Devonshire was completed by John Lane, stonemason at Hardwick Hall, in 1981.

Samson and Delilah by Tintoretto (1518–94) is on the wall of the last flight of steps. A painting of Chatsworth as it was in Bess of Hardwick's time is next to another by William Marlow showing the house as rebuilt (1686–1707) by the 1st Duke of Devonshire, and the stables added (1758–63) by the 4th Duke. A third painting of Chatsworth in the time of the 3rd Duke, by Smith of Derby, was bought in 1983. The picture at the foot of the stairs, *Large Interior, London, W.9,* (painted 1973) is by Lucian Freud.

The doorways on all three floors were originally windows giving directly onto the court, providing more light than there is now. They lead to corridors which, like the Sketch Galleries, were added by the 6th Duke to make it easier to move round the house.

The wrought iron panels on the landings are by Jean Tijou and incorporate the initials C (Cavendish) and D (Devonshire) with ducal coronets. They were originally made for the Great Stairs but were later incorporated into the balustrade, which was made by

Detail from *An Allegory of Peace* by Simon Vouet (1590–1649)

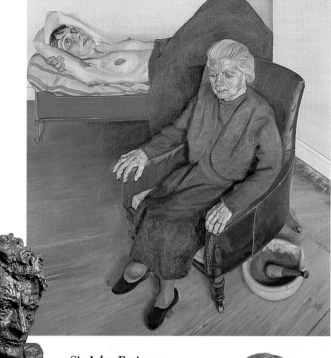

The present Duke of Devonshire continues the family tradition of collecting and has acquired many works of art over the last forty years. His particular interests are fine illustrated books, minerals, and paintings, drawings and sculpture by recent and contemporary artists. Of the works of the two artists illustrated on this page, the Duke writes 'Both the collection of pictures by Lucian Freud and the sculpture by Angela Conner are the results of my long-standing friendship with the artists. In both cases I was drawn to their work by my affection for them, hence the various commissions of portraits of family and friends'.

11th Duke of Devonshire

Sir John Betjeman
(1906–84)

Right:
Lucian Freud (*b.* 1922) and above, his painting *Large Interior, W.9.*

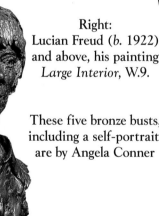

These five bronze busts, including a self-portrait, are by Angela Conner

HRH
The Prince of Wales
(*b.* 1948)

THE WEST CORRIDOR

On the left as you enter the corridor is an Egyptian stele, or memorial tablet, of the 11th dynasty (2040–1991 B.C.) and on the right is another, smaller one of the same period. The mutilated marble torso is from the Holy Land and dates from the late 12th century, a rare example from the 'Crusader' period. The stalactites under the table of Derbyshire fossil-limestone are from Castleton, 14 miles away.

Across the courtyard you get the best view of the trophies carved in stone by Watson and the passages designed by Wyatville which were added on

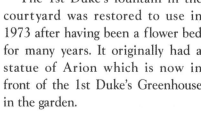

the other three sides in the 19th century. Samuel Watson from Heanor, Derbyshire, came to Chatsworth in 1689 and worked here, in wood and stone, almost continuously, until his death in 1715.

The 1st Duke's fountain in the courtyard was restored to use in 1973 after having been a flower bed for many years. It originally had a statue of Arion which is now in front of the 1st Duke's Greenhouse in the garden.

Memorial tablet of *Renu and his wife Dedet*, Egyptian, 11th Dynasty

THE CHAPEL

The chapel was built between 1688 and 1693 and has remained unaltered ever since. If the 1st Duke could return to Chatsworth he would immediately recognise his creation. Laguerre and Ricard painted the walls and ceilings with scenes from the life of Christ, restored by Pauline Plummer and her team 1985–88. Verrio painted *Doubting Thomas* over the altar. The two large flanking figures were executed by Cibber, the designer of the whole. Samuel Watson and his assistants from London carved the altar-piece of local alabaster. The lime wood carvings are traditionally ascribed to Grinling Gibbons (1648–1721) and could have been sent up from London.

The four black marble columns were hewn from a single block quarried on Sheldon Moor, a few miles away. The strong smell comes from the cedar wainscot, and not from incense as many people think. Hanging from the gallery is the Garter Banner of the 10th Duke (1895–1950) from the chapel of the Order, St. George's Chapel, Windsor. The pair of huge brass candlesticks was bought for £60 in London in 1691. The needlework seats and backs of the tall chairs were worked in *gros point* for the 6th Duke by friends and relations whose names are painted on them. The chairs themselves are 17th century. The sister of the present (11th) Duke, Lady Anne Cavendish was married in the Chapel to Mr. Michael Tree in 1949.

Ceiling painting, *c.* 1690, showing
Christ in Glory, by Louis Laguerre (1663–1721)

Sketch for one of the
carvings in the Chapel
attributed to Grinling Gibbons
(1648–1721)

Lime wood carving
attributed to
Grinling Gibbons
(1648–1721)

THE OAK ROOM

An Italian torchère, walnut, late 17th century, in the form of a winged figure of Atlas, supporting a Victorian bracket clock by John Smith of Derby

This is certainly the oddest room in the house. The oak panelling and carved heads are from a German monastery and were bought by the 6th Duke on an impulse, having been tempted into an auction room in Berners Street, London. Before it was altered, this room contained some of the 12,000 volumes of the library of Henry Cavendish (1731–1810) the scientist. The opening from the Chapel was made in 1960, to ease the circulation of summer visitors.

Many of the smaller pieces of oriental china in the collection are in the cupboards round the room. Inset into the panelling between the windows are paintings of some of the 6th Duke's favourite dogs.

The 6th Duke gives his own account (1844) of the various uses to which this room was put: "It was the dormitory of poor Dicky Smith, the Chaplain; and to this room I remember banishing the learned Parr, when he insisted on having a room to smoke in – a desire then (1813) considered most atrocious and derogatory. Of late years, when family prayers have been read this has been the suitable place for them; and when the Grand Duke Michael Paulowitsch arrived on a visit last year at a very late hour here he had the gayest-looking supper which contrasted agreeably with the dingy walls, and looked like a jolly friar's repast".

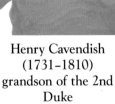

Henry Cavendish (1731–1810) grandson of the 2nd Duke

THE CHAPEL PASSAGE

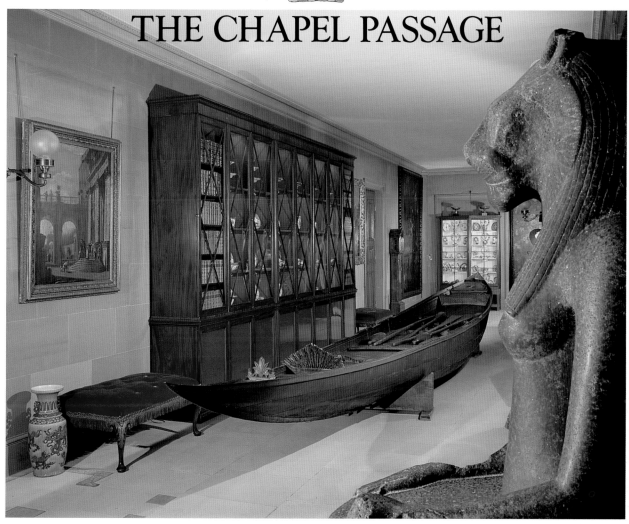

ow you are back in the Chapel Passage. The Turkish barge was given to the 6th Duke for his use on the Bosphorus by the Sultan of Turkey in 1839. The two ancient Egyptian statues of the goddess Sekhmet were moved here from the garden in 1991. They come from the temple of Mut at Karnak and date from the 18th Dynasty (1570–1304 B.C.). On the inner wall hangs *The Adoration of the Magi* by Paolo Veronese (c.1528–88). The colossal foot, long thought to be a 19th century fake, has now been identified as part of a gigantic Greek statue, dating from the time of Christ. The other foot is in a Berlin museum. In the showcase are presentation keys used at opening ceremonies and on the lower shelves are 18th century toy silver furniture and tableware.

Left:
Collection of house keys

Below:
Colossal foot, Greek, 1st century A.D.

A bas-relief of *Diana Bathing*,
bought in London in 1692

Opposite:
The Painted Hall looking North

THE GROTTO

The Grotto supports the Great Stairs above. It was built to contain the lowest flight of stairs, moved, on second thoughts, to the Painted Hall. Because it was so dark and dreary, the 1st Duke decided on its elaborate decoration. The bas-relief of *Diana Bathing* above the fountain on the south wall was bought in 1692. Its marble frame and basin below it, the swags of flowers in Roche Abbey stone and the Garter Stars in the ceiling were all carved by Samuel Watson.

The showcases contain gifts received by the present Duke and Duchess on official occasions, and decorations bestowed on Mary Duchess of Devonshire (1895–1988) when she was Mistress of the Robes to Her Majesty the Queen from 1953 to 1966.

Returning through the Painted Hall you pass a group of marble busts, most of which are Roman, 1st–3rd century A.D.

A colossal bust of *Antinous Dionysus*,
Roman, 2nd century A.D.

36

THE OAK STAIRS

This staircase was built by Wyatville in 1823–4 to give access to his new wing, begun in 1818. The dome and lantern were completed in 1829. In 1928 Evelyn Duchess of Devonshire, and the architect W. H. Romaine-Walker attempted to disguise Wyatville's work as that of the time of William and Mary by putting in old doors and adding surrounds and a cornice in the style of the State Rooms. The brown brocade and stippled walls (plaster painted to look like stone) also date from 1928. The chandelier of stags' horns from Windsor Park was originally in the Theatre and was hung here in 1959. The horns were a gift to the 6th Duke from William IV.

Limewood carving of lace cravat, woodcock, leaves and a portrait medallion by Grinling Gibbons (1648–1721)

Right:
The oak staircase built by Wyatville in 1823–4

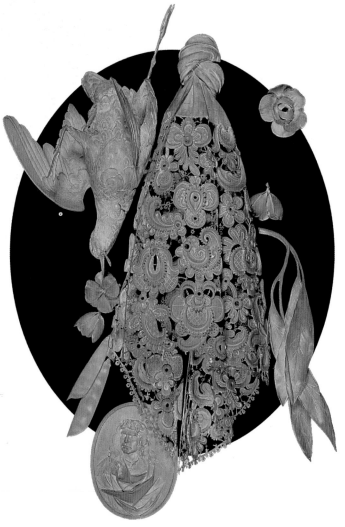

The 6th Duke of Devonshire by Sir George Hayter (1792–1871)

The large equestrian portrait, c. 1675, of Lord William Cavendish, later 4th Earl and 1st Duke, is by Vandermeulen, (1632-90). He had accompanied an embassy to France and is shown dressed in the height of French fashion.

The portrait by Hayter of the 6th Duke was given to the present Duke by Derby Borough Council when their Guildhall became a theatre in the 1970s. Opposite is a portrait of King George IV from the studio of Sir Thomas Lawrence (1769-1830).

In a case is a virtuoso example of a Grinling Gibbons (1648-1721) carving. It includes a portrait medallion possibly of the artist.

King George IV
by Sir Thomas Lawrence
1769-1830

Below: *King Henry VIII*
A portrait after the original by
Hans Holbein (1497/8–1543)

The Library, c. 1827,
watercolour by William Henry
Hunt (1790–1864)

THE LIBRARY

Originally this room was the 1st Duke's Long Gallery. The ceiling of gilded stucco by Edward Goudge, with paintings by Verrio, survives from this time and its design is reflected in the Axminster carpet which was woven when the room was altered.

In 1815 the 6th Duke fitted the room out as a library. He bought several complete collections of books to add to the many he inherited and he and Wyatville designed the present gallery and bookcases to receive them, *c.* 1830. There are over 17,000 volumes in here and in the Ante-Library.

In 1983 the paintwork and gilding of the Library were restored. The sofas and chairs were at Devonshire House and the cut-velvet curtains were hung *c.* 1830.

An illuminated
manuscript from the
Library

Ceiling painting of *Iris presenting the wounded Venus to Mars* by Sir George Hayter (1792–1871)

THE ANTE-LIBRARY

The Ante-Library contains some of the thousands of books to be found throughout the house. The bookcases are made of mahogany and brass like those in the Library. The ceiling painting was the Royal Academy picture of the year in 1823, *Iris presenting the wounded Venus to Mars*, by Sir George Hayter (1792–1871). The mahogany writing-table was designed by William Kent (1685–1748) for his friend and patron Lord Burlington about 1730.

An illuminated manuscript from the Library

Palissy-ware dish, late 16th century

THE DOME ROOM

This is where the 1st Duke's house ends and the 6th Duke's wing begins. The two vases are made of a very rare marble, *occhio di paone*, and are the first of many examples in this part of the house of the 6th Duke's passion for stone.

The open book displayed in the case is a volume from the set of John James Audubon's *Birds of America* (1827–38) which in its day was the largest and grandest book ever printed. The ivory chess set, with chessmen in the shape of elephants, juggernauts and pagodas, is Indian. The incorrect positions of some pieces is determined by pegs which hold them in place.

Roseate spoonbill from *The Birds of America*
by John James Audubon (1785–1851)

Pieces from the ivory chess set,
Indian, early 19th century

THE GREAT DINING ROOM

So called to distinguish it from the State Dining Room and three other dining rooms in the house, this is the first important room of Wyatville's wing. When it was finished in 1832, the 6th Duke wrote 'It answers perfectly, never feeling overlarge . . . It is like dining in a great trunk and you expect the lid to open'. It was used by the family until 1939 and redecorated and hung with crimson material in 1996.

The four heavy gilt pier tables were made for the room. The glass lights on the walls were at Devonshire House, put up here in 1959, having been in packing cases for 40 years. The marble fireplaces and bacchanalian figures were carved by Sir Richard Westmacott the Younger (1799–1872) and Robert Sievier (1794–1865). The 6th Duke was disappointed with them; 'I wanted more abandon and joyous expression' he wrote.

The first dinner given in this room was for Princess Victoria when she stayed here with her mother, the Duchess of Kent, in 1832. The Princess was 13 and it was the first time she dined with grown-up people. There was a cooked rehearsal the night before. Most of the large pieces of silver, commissioned by the 6th Duke for use at banquets, are by Paul Storr (1771–1844) and Robert Garrard (1793–1881).

Giltwood centre table, *c.* 1830.
On the table are a pair of silver candelabra 1813–14, by Paul Storr (1771–1844); a silver sideboard dish embossed with a scene of *Perseus turning Phineus to stone*, made in Rome, 18th century; a pair of silver tureens, 1755–56, by Frederick Kandler and a silver entree dish, 1806, by Richard Cooke

The Great Dining Room

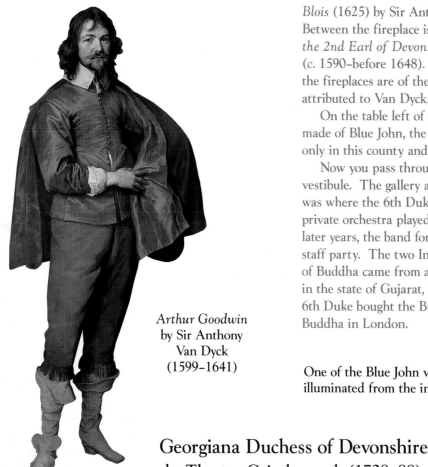

Arthur Goodwin
by Sir Anthony
Van Dyck
(1599–1641)

The portraits left and right of the door as you enter are of *Arthur Goodwin* (1639) and *Jeanne de Blois* (1625) by Sir Anthony Van Dyck (1599–1641). Between the fireplace is *The Widow and Children of the 2nd Earl of Devonshire* by Daniel Mytens (*c.* 1590–before 1648). The portraits on the right of the fireplaces are of the 3rd Earl and his wife attributed to Van Dyck.

On the table left of the far door is a pair of vases made of Blue John, the Derbyshire fluorspar mined only in this county and first worked by the Romans.

Now you pass through the vestibule. The gallery above was where the 6th Duke's private orchestra played and, in later years, the band for the annual staff party. The two Indian statues of Buddha came from a Jain temple in the state of Gujarat, and the 6th Duke bought the Burmese Buddha in London.

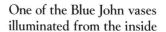

One of the Blue John vases
illuminated from the inside

Georgiana Duchess of Devonshire
by Thomas Gainsborough (1728–88)

On 13th July 1994 the Chatsworth House Trust bought this portrait at Sotheby's. All but forgotten in recent years, a century ago it was one of the most famous paintings in the world.

The portrait was painted as a whole-length *c.* 1785–8 but its owner in the 1830s, an elderly schoolmistress called Miss Maginnis, cut it down to fit over her fireplace. In 1841 she sold it to a picture dealer, John Bentley, who later gave it to his friend the collector Wynn Ellis. Ellis died in 1875 and part of his collection was sent for sale at Christie's.

In the week before the sale on 6th May 1876 the Duchess's portrait became the talk of the town. Some doubted that it was by Gainsborough, others that it was of the Duchess of Devonshire, but all were enchanted by its beauty.

It was bought by William Agnew, the Bond Street dealer, for 10,100 guineas – the highest price ever paid for a picture up to that date. This increased the picture's fame, but the greatest sensation was to come.

On 26th May 1876 the picture was cut from its stretcher during the night and stolen. The thief was a notorious international crook, Adam Worth, alias Harry Raymond – believed now to have been Sir Arthur Conan Doyle's model for the sinister Moriarty in the Sherlock Holmes stories. Worth and a friend,

Jack Phillips, intended to blackmail Agnew's into putting up a bond to secure the release from prison of Worth's brother.

Despite demands from the thief, and the receipt by post of strips of canvas cut from the painting, Agnew's refused to comply and the story petered out. Not until 1901, following a tip-off and the payment of a reward, was the portrait recovered for Agnew's by Pinkerton Agents in Chicago.

The picture was then bought by the famous American millionaire collector Pierpont Morgan and remained in his family until 1994. It has since been cleaned and some later retouchings and varnishes removed.

Many portraits of the Duchess were painted but her face in this one does not closely resemble any of them, giving rise to the doubts expressed in 1876. There is, however, a small monochrome copy of it (now in the National Gallery of Art, Washington D.C.) painted before the original was cut down and always identified as Georgiana by her descendants who owned it. New technical evidence suggests that parts of the face may have been re-worked by Gainsborough or another artist not long after him. The evidence confirms, though, that the original portrait is by Gainsborough himself.

THE SCULPTURE GALLERY

The 6th Duke indulged his love of stone and sculpted figures in this room which he built to display his collection of what was then modern sculpture. On the left as you enter is the *Discobolus*, by Matthaus Kessels (1784–1836). *The Spinning Girl*, of 1819, is by Rudolf Schadow (1786–1822) and *The Wounded Achilles*, by Filippo Albacini (1777–1858). On the right is *Mars restrained by Cupid* by John Gibson (1786–1866), *Ganymede and the Eagle of Jove* by Adamo Tadolini (1788–1868), *Hebe, Cup-bearer to the Gods* and *The Sleeping Endymion with his Dog* by Antonio Canova (1757–1822).

For the group of *Mars and Cupid*, Gibson needed an exceptionally large block of the best Carrara marble, which was finally delivered at his studio in Rome drawn by twenty buffaloes and with 'the whole town out to watch'. The round bas-reliefs on the walls are *Day* on the right and *Night* opposite, by Bertel Thorvaldsen (c.1770–1844). The rectangular reliefs on the right of scenes from the legend of Achilles are by the same sculptor, and those on the left, by Schadow, show rape and battle scenes from the story of Castor and Pollux.

Above:
Details from *Day* and *Night*,
bas-reliefs by Bertel
Thorvaldsen (*c.* 1770–1844)

Hebe, Cup-bearer to the Gods by Antonio Canova (1757–1822)

The Sleeping Endymion with his Dog by Antonio Canova (1757–1822)

In the middle of the Gallery, Napoleon's sister, Princess Pauline Borghese, by Campbell, and his mother by Canova, (bought in 1818), sit in their white marble chairs. These and Endymion were among the most treasured purchases of the 6th Duke. He admired Canova above all other sculptors. Later in the 19th century, these works went out of fashion. Now they are sought after once more and a major exhibition of neo-classical art in London in 1972 put them back in the public eye. A portrait of Canova after Lawrence hangs between the tapestries on the right.

In 1990 eight more pieces of sculpture were returned to the Sculpture Gallery, from whence they were removed at various times during the previous eighty years. The group of *Paris and Oenone*, 1848, in the centre of the gallery is by Ludwig Michael von Schwanthaler (1802–48), who called it his swansong because it was the last work he completed before he died. In the central bay on the right (east) wall are two recumbent figures, *A Bacchante* by Lorenzo Bartolini (1777–1850), commissioned by the Duke in 1822, and *Venus with Cupid removing a thorn from her foot*, 1825, by Pietro Tenerani (1789–1869). On the west wall is *The Cymbal Player*, 1832, by Richard Westmacott the Younger (1799–1872). Near it is a head by Canova of *Napoleon's mother, Letizia Bonaparte*, bought by the Duke in 1823.

The two massive lions either side of the door to the Orangery were the bulkiest removals. They are copies of those by Canova which form part of the Rezzonico Monument in St. Peter's, Rome. The *Sleeping Lion* is by Rinaldo Rinaldi (1793–1873) and the *Crouching Lion* (which weighs 3½ tons) by Francesco Benaglia. They were commissioned by the 6th Duke in 1823. For many years they were out of doors, flanking the steps from the Orangery into the garden. Now they are back in their original positions. The busts in the niches high up each side of the entrance door are of *Canova* by Rinaldo Rinaldi (1793–1873) and *The 6th Duke* by Thomas Campbell

Crouching Lion by Francesco Benaglia

Bust of *Napoleon* by Antonio Canova

Napoleon's Mother by Antonio Canova

The sculptor *Canova* by Rinaldo Rinaldi (1793–1873)

(1790–1858). Nearby, against the right (east) wall, is another copy of Canova's work, a bronze statue of *The Penitent Magdalen*.

The tapestries are Brussels, of mythological subjects, woven by Cobus and Coenot *c*. 1690.

In the last part of the Gallery on the left wall are two portraits by Frans Hals (*c*. 1582/3–1666). Between them is *Portrait of an Oriental* (believed to be King Uzziah stricken by leprosy) by Rembrandt (1606–69). Opposite is Sir Edwin Landseer's *Trial by Jury*, sometimes called *Laying Down the Law*, painted in 1840. This is a satire on the legal profession and the poodle may represent Lord Lyndhurst, the Lord Chancellor of the day. The Blenheim spaniel on the left of the picture is the 6th Duke's own pet dog 'Bony' specially added as a 'cub reporter'. Other paintings on this wall are by Bernardo Strozzi (1581–1644), Valentin de Boulogne (1594–1632), William Collins (1788–1847) and James Carmichael (1800–68).

The gritstone walls of The Sculpture Gallery were hung with red and green velvet in the 1960s to give a more definite background to the sculptures. The gasoliers, now electrified, were bought from Wanstead in Essex when the contents of that house were sold in 1822. The doorstops are sawn-off models of Paxton's Great Conservatory, which formerly stood in the Garden.

Left:
Portrait of a man
by Frans Hals
(1582/3–1666)

Right:
Portrait of a woman
by Frans Hals

Below:
Trial by Jury by Sir Edwin Landseer
(1802–73)

Below:
Sleeping Lion
by Rinaldo Rinaldi
(1793–1873) after
Canova

Portrait of an Oriental
believed to be
King Uzziah stricken by leprosy

Rembrandt
1606–69

The panel is signed and dated, very indistinctly, *Rembran f. 1639.* (?)
It was bought for £78:15:0 by the 3rd Duke of Devonshire in 1742

THE ORANGERY SHOP

The 6th Duke's plan for the north wing was to end with the Sculpture Gallery but when he got 'bit by gardening' due to the enthusiasm engendered by his head gardener and friend Joseph Paxton (1803–65), the Orangery was added. More sculpture and tender plants shared it happily for years. Now it contains a shop, but there is still room for a copy by Lorenzo Bartolini (1777–1850) of the Medici Vase and several remaining marble busts and statues by neo-classical sculptors.

When the house re-opened in 1949 guide books and the sickly-sweet Chatsworth bon-bons, sold from a wheelbarrow, were all that was offered for sale. By the 1960s part of the Orangery had been arranged as a shop and the range began to grow. Today you can see a wide variety of gifts, many selected by the Duchess of Devonshire and some based on designs from the house and garden. The profits go towards the upkeep of the House.

Here ends the tour of the house. You have walked over a third of a mile and have climbed 100 steps up and 60 steps down since you went through the gates of the porter's lodge.

A small selection of the gifts available from the Orangery Shop

THE GARDEN

Through the Orangery doors lies the garden, with over 100 acres and 5 miles of footpaths to explore. This is another story and has its own guide book.

THE CASCADE HOUSE

One of the principal features of the 1st Duke's Garden was the Cascade. Finished in 1696 it was rebuilt only five years later on a grander scale. It was designed by a Frenchman, Grillet, a pupil of the celebrated Le Nôtre. The Temple or Cascade House was added in 1703 to the plans of Thomas Archer, the Warwickshire architect. The stone carving is by Nadauld and Samuel Watson.

Aerial view of Chatsworth
from the Hunting Tower

The Hunting Tower
with rhododendrons in bloom

THE CAVENDISH FAMILY

1505-1557 Sir William Cavendish = Bess of Hardwick c. 1527-1608
son of Thomas Cavendish of Suffolk   later Countess of Shrewsbury

1552-1625 William Cavendish = Anne Keighley d. 1625
1st Earl of Devonshire (1618)   *dau. of Henry Keighley*

1590-1628 William Cavendish = Hon. Christian Bruce 1595-1675
2nd Earl of Devonshire   *dau. of 1st Lord Kinloss*

1617-1684 William Cavendish = Lady Elizabeth Cecil 1619-1689
3rd Earl of Devonshire   *dau. of the 2nd Earl of Salisbury*

1640-1707 William Cavendish = Lady Mary Butler 1646-1710
4th Earl of Devonshire   *dau. of the 1st Duke*
1st Duke of Devonshire (1694)   *of Ormonde*

1673-1729 William Cavendish = Hon. Rachel Russell 1674-1725
2nd Duke of Devonshire   *dau. of William Lord Russell*

1698-1755 William Cavendish = Catherine Hoskins d. 1777
3rd Duke of Devonshire   *dau. of John Hoskins*

Lord Charles Cavendish = Lady Anne Grey d. 1733
d. 1783   *dau. of the Duke of Kent*

1720-1764 William Cavendish = Lady Charlotte Boyle 1731-1754
4th Duke of Devonshire   *dau. of the 4th Earl of Cork and 3rd Earl of Burlington; estates in Yorkshire and Ireland, Chiswick House, Burlington House*

1731-1810 Henry Cavendish *the scientist*

1757-1806(1) Lady Georgiana Spencer = William Cavendish 1748-1811 = (2) Lady Elizabeth Foster
dau. of the 1st Earl Spencer   5th Duke of Devonshire   *(née Hervey) 1757-1824 dau. of the 4th Earl of Bristol*

1754-1834 Lord George = Lady Elizabeth Compton
Cavendish   *1760-1835 heiress to the 7th*
1st Earl of Burlington   *Earl of Northampton;*
(2nd creation)   *estates in Sussex*

1790-1858 William Spencer Cavendish
6th Duke of Devonshire

Lady Georgiana Cavendish = George Howard 1773-1848
1783-1858   6th Earl of Carlisle

1783-1812 William Cavendish = Hon. Louisa O'Callaghan
killed in carriage accident   d. 1863 dau. of the 1st Lord Lismore

1803-1881 Lady Caroline Howard = Rt. Hon. William Lascelles 1798-1851
son of the 2nd Earl of Harewood

1812-1840 Lady Blanche Howard = William Cavendish 1808-1891
2nd Earl of Burlington (2nd creation)
7th Duke of Devonshire

1838-1920 Emma Lascelles = Lord Edward Cavendish 1838-1891

1833-1908 Spencer Compton Cavendish = Countess Louise von Alten 1832-1911
8th Duke of Devonshire   *"The Double Duchess"; formerly Duchess of Manchester*

1868-1938 Victor Cavendish = Lady Evelyn Fitzmaurice 1870-1960
9th Duke of Devonshire   *dau. of the 5th Marquess of Lansdowne*

1895-1950 Edward Cavendish = Lady Mary Cecil 1895-1988
10th Duke of Devonshire   *dau. of the 4th Marquess of Salisbury*

b. 1920 Andrew Cavendish = Hon. Deborah Mitford *b.* 1920
11th Duke of Devonshire   *dau. of the 2nd Lord Redesdale*

1917-1944 William Cavendish = Kathleen Kennedy 1920-1948
Marquess of Hartington   sister of President Kennedy
killed in action

b. 1944 Peregrine Cavendish = Amanda Heywood-Lonsdale
Marquess of Hartington   b. 1944

Lady Emma Cavendish = Hon. Tobias Tennant
b. 1943   *son of the 2nd Lord Glenconner*

Lady Sophia Cavendish = (1) Anthony Murphy
b. 1957   (2) Alastair Morrison

b. 1969 William Cavendish
Earl of Burlington

Lady Celina Cavendish
b. 1971

Lady Jasmine Cavendish
b. 1973

Isabel Tennant
b. 1964

Edward Tennant
b. 1967

Stella Tennant
b. 1970

Declan Morrison
b. 1993

Nancy Morrison
b. 1995

THE HISTORY OF THE HOUSE AND THE CAVENDISH FAMILY

The first house at Chatsworth was built by 'Bess of Hardwick' (c. 1527–1608) and her second husband Sir William Cavendish (1505-57). Building began in 1552 and continued for many years. The Hunting Tower, which stands on the escarpment to the east, is of the 1580s. Bess had four husbands but she only had children by Sir William. Their second son, William, became the heir and was created Earl of Devonshire in 1618.

Sir William Cavendish came from Cavendish in Suffolk. He prospered in the service of Henry VIII as one of the King's commissioners for the dissolution of the monasteries. When he married the redoubtable Bess, who was a native of Derbyshire, she persuaded him to sell the former monastery lands he owned elsewhere and move to her home county. In spite of the physical limitations of the site, which was prone to flooding and difficult of access across the moors to the east, they built a large house on the site of the square block of the present building. There is a painting of the house which hangs at the bottom of the West Stairs, so we know what it looked like outside, but there is nothing to tell us what the interior was like, although an inventory of 1601 survives, attached to Bess's will.

Elizabethan Chatsworth
by Richard Wilson (1713–82)
after a lost original

Bess of Hardwick
(c. 1527–1608) and her
second husband *Sir William
Cavendish* (1505–57)

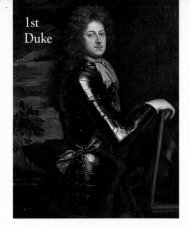

1st Duke

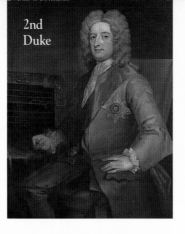

2nd Duke

3rd Duke

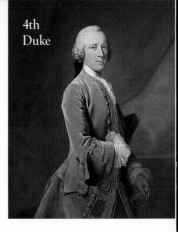

4th Duke

After Sir William died in 1557 Bess married Sir William St. Loe (*d.* 1565) and lastly, in 1567, George Talbot, 6th Earl of Shrewsbury (*c.* 1528-90). Queen Elizabeth I appointed Shrewsbury custodian of Mary Queen of Scots, who was a prisoner at Chatsworth at various times between 1569 and 1584. Her lodgings were on the east side of the house and the rooms there, though changed beyond recognition, are still called the Queen of Scots Apartments. Bess died in 1608. She also built Hardwick Hall, near Chesterfield, her surviving masterpiece. It belonged to the Cavendish family until 1957 when it was taken by the government in lieu of death duty and given by them to the National Trust.

Few alterations were made at Chatsworth until near the end of the 17th century. In 1686 the 4th Earl (1640-1707; created 1st Duke of Devonshire in 1694 for his part in bringing William of Orange to the English throne) began to pull down the South Front. He intended to alter only this part of the house but he found building so delightful that once he started he could not stop. The East Front followed, and he spent three years erecting new outbuildings. George London and Henry Wise designed a formal garden on the grand scale. A Frenchman, Grillet, built the cascade, and Thomas Archer (1668-1743) designed the house from which it springs. Leendert Knyff was commissioned to make a drawing to record the changes but hardly was this done when the desire to build again proved irresistible. The Duke rebuilt the West Front (1699-1702) and then the remaining North Front. The Canal Pond was dug where once there was a hill (1702). William Talman (1650-1720) was the architect for the South and East Fronts. The West was perhaps designed by the Duke himself and the North by Thomas Archer. The new Chatsworth was finished just before the Duke died in 1707.

The 2nd Duke (1673-1729) made no changes to the house and garden he had watched being created in his youth. He made his mark in a different field, as a collector of paintings, drawings and prints. He also made important collections of coins and carved Greek and Roman gems. The 2nd Duke was the grandfather of Henry Cavendish (1731-1810), the distinguished and eccentric scientist, who determined the composition of water, recognised hydrogen as an element and was 'the first man to weigh the world'. Cavendish's library of 12,000 books on science and many other subjects is at Chatsworth.

The 3rd Duke (1698-1755) served for seven years as Lord Lieutenant of Ireland and was Member of Parliament from 1721 till his father's death sent him to the House of Lords in 1729. Sir Robert Walpole, the Prime Minister, was a friend of his and his father, and the two Van Dyck portraits of Arthur Goodwin and Jeanne de Blois, which hang in the Great Dining Room, came from Walpole's collection. When Devonshire House in Piccadilly was burnt down in 1733, the 3rd Duke commissioned William Kent to rebuild it. Kent designed furniture for it, much of which is now at Chatsworth.

The 4th Duke (1720-64) was a prominent Whig politician like his father, serving as Lord Lieutenant of Ireland, and from November 1756 to May 1757 as Prime Minister of England. He made great changes to the park and garden. He decided that the house should be approached from the west, so he pulled down the old stables and offices which interfered with the view on this side, and razed the cottages of Edensor village which were visible from the house. The architect James Paine (*c.* 1716-89) was commissioned to build new stables up the slope to the north-east (completed 1763). The course of the river was altered and Paine designed a new bridge upstream of the house (1762). Land to the west of the river, and what remained of Edensor village was enclosed to become the park as it is today. Lancelot ('Capability') Brown (1716-83) was engaged to destroy most of the 1st Duke's formal garden and to give the park the natural, romantic look which he had helped bring into fashion.

The 4th Duke married Lady Charlotte Boyle, only surviving daughter and heiress of the 3rd Earl of Burlington, the architect and connoisseur. This marriage brought new estates to the Cavendish family, including Lismore Castle in County Waterford, Londesborough Hall and Bolton Abbey in Yorkshire, Burlington House and Chiswick House in London. The inheritance included all Lord Burlington's architectural books and drawings as well as many paintings and everything else his houses contained.

The 5th Duke (1748-1811) married Lady Georgiana Spencer, famous for her charm and beloved by all who knew her. She and her great friend Lady Elizabeth Foster were painted several times by Sir Joshua Reynolds and Thomas Gainsborough. Lady Elizabeth became the mistress of the Duke, and had

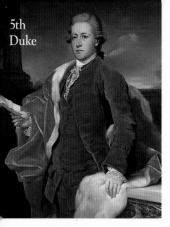

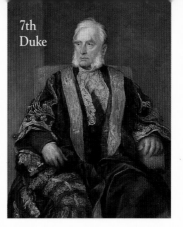

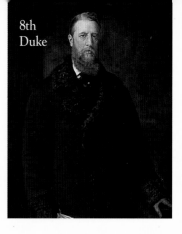

two children by him, but curiously enough this did not interfere with her friendship with Georgiana. The *ménage à trois* continued for some years and has been the subject of many books.

The 5th Duke and Georgiana lived mostly in London but when they did come to Chatsworth they filled it with friends and relations, writers and politicians. The house was open for people to see round and on one day a month dinner was provided for whoever came. John Carr of York (1723-1807) was commissioned by the Duke to redesign the decoration and furnishings of the private drawing rooms of the first floor at Chatsworth and build the Crescent in Buxton.

There were three children of the marriage. The eldest, Georgiana, married the 6th Earl of Carlisle and became the mother of Lady Blanche Howard who married her cousin William, who eventually became the 7th Duke of Devonshire.

The 6th, the 'Bachelor' Duke (1790-1858), was Duchess Georgiana's only son and succeeded his father at the age of 21. Extravagant and charming, he was a prince of hosts. He never married but loved entertaining his friends and spent 47 years improving his many houses and collecting objects of every kind with which to embellish them. He bought two complete libraries, many paintings and sculptures and a great deal more besides. He engaged the architect Sir Jeffry Wyatville (1766-1840) to build the long North Wing at Chatsworth. Later, Lismore Castle in County Waterford was rebuilt too. Such expenditure taxed even his resources and he was forced to sell property in Yorkshire, including most of the town of Wetherby and his estate at Londesborough.

He became intensely interested in gardening after he met Joseph Paxton (1803-65), a young gardener working in the Horticultural Society's gardens at Chiswick which adjoined the Duke's land there. He appointed Paxton to be head gardener at Chatsworth in 1826 and together they changed the garden into the one you see today. Expeditions were sent to the Americas and the Far East to collect plants, giant rockeries were introduced and the 'Conservative Wall' glasshouse was built. Paxton designed and constructed the Emperor Fountain, the jet in the Canal Pond which can reach over 280 feet on a calm day. It was an engineering feat which entailed draining the moor

into an eight acre man-made reservoir on the high ground above the house (1844). The whole of this ambitious scheme was completed in six months.

However, the most famous of Paxton's achievements was the building of the Great Conservatory, constructed in wood, iron and glass and covering three-quarters of an acre. It was the forerunner of the Crystal Palace, which he built for the Great Exhibition of 1851 in Hyde Park. Sadly, the Great Conservatory became derelict during the First World War and was demolished soon after.

The 6th Duke died in 1858. He was succeeded by William Cavendish, 2nd Earl of Burlington of the second creation (1808-91), the grandson of the 6th Duke's uncle Lord George Cavendish. The 7th Duke married Lady Blanche Howard, granddaughter of Duchess Georgiana. Blanche died aged 29 in 1840 and was mourned by her husband and her uncle for the rest of their lives. He was a scholar, Second Wrangler and Smith's Prizewinner in mathematics, Chancellor of London University at the age of 28, and later Chancellor of Cambridge University and founder of the Cavendish Laboratory there.

Chatsworth was a very quiet place during the thirty years of the 7th Duke's tenure, as its owner decreed strict economies after the extravagance of his predecessor. He is best remembered today as the developer of Eastbourne in Sussex and Barrow-in-Furness in Cumbria. His son the 8th Duke (1833-1908) was a statesman who served in Parliament for over fifty years. He was a towering figure in the Liberal Party and as Marquess of Hartington he played a leading rôle in the cabinets of Gladstone and later Liberal governments. Three times he was asked by Queen Victoria to become Prime Minister, but each time he refused. In 1886 he split the Liberal Party over his opposition to Home Rule for Ireland. He married Louise, widow of the Duke of Manchester, in 1892. They had no children.

They entertained lavishly at Chatsworth, usually during the autumn and winter. King Edward VII and Queen Alexandra were regular visitors. In 1908 the Duke died and was succeeded by his nephew Victor Cavendish.

The 9th Duke (1868-1938) and his wife Lady Evelyn Fitzmaurice, daughter of the 5th Marquess of

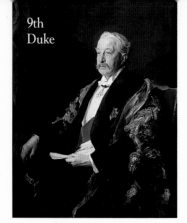

9th
Duke

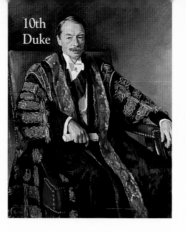

10th
Duke

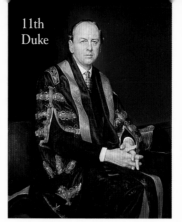

11th
Duke

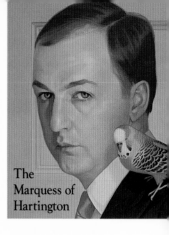

The
Marquess of
Hartington

Lansdowne (Viceroy of India 1888–1894), had seven children. He was a Member of Parliament from 1891 and like most of his predecessors loved politics and continued to attend the House of Lords after the death of his uncle. He held office as Financial Secretary to the Treasury and from 1916 to 1921 was Governor-General of Canada.

When the Duke and Duchess moved to Chatsworth in 1908 a lot of work had to be done to the house, including the complete renewal of the drainage system. Evelyn Duchess herself interested in the collections and became very knowledgeable about the contents of the various houses, while her husband was an attentive landlord and enjoyed his farming and sporting activities. The 9th Duke was the first to have to pay death duties, which amounted to over half a million pounds. Added to the even greater running debt left by the failure of the 7th Duke's business ventures, this forced some major sales. All the Caxton books in the library and the John Kemble collection of plays, including many rare first editions of Shakespeare, were sold in 1912 to the Huntington Library in California, and Devonshire House and its three acres in Piccadilly were sold in 1920.

When Edward Cavendish (1895–1950) succeeded his father as 10th Duke in 1938 he and his wife, Lady Mary Cecil, daughter of the 4th Marquess of Salisbury, planned to make many alterations and improvements at Chatsworth. But a year later, war broke out and the girls and staff of Penrhos College arrived. The house was not re-opened to the public until 1949.

The 10th Duke's elder son William, Marquess of Hartington (b. 1917), married Kathleen Kennedy, sister of the late President Kennedy, in May 1944. Four months later he was killed in action in Belgium while serving with his regiment, the Coldstream Guards. Kathleen died in an aeroplane accident in 1948. They had no children, so the Duke's second son Andrew Cavendish became his father's heir and succeeded to the title in 1950.

Andrew Robert Buxton Cavendish, M.C., P.C., 11th Duke of Devonshire (b. 1920) married the Hon. Deborah Mitford, daughter of Lord Redesdale, in 1941. He served in the Coldstream Guards during the war, and was Mayor of Buxton 1952–54. Later he was a minister in the Conservative government 1960–64. The Duke and Duchess have three children, Emma (b. 1943), Peregrine, Marquess of Hartington (b. 1944) and Sophia

(b. 1957). Lady Emma married the Hon. Toby Tennant in 1963 and they have three children. Lady Sophia married Alastair Morrison in 1988 and they have two children. Lord Hartington married Amanda Heywood-Lonsdale (b. 1944) in 1967 and they have three children, William, Earl of Burlington (b.1969), Celina (b. 1971) and Jasmine (b. 1973).

The 10th Duke's death at the age of 55 was sudden and unexpected, and death duties at the maximum rate of 80% had to be paid. Nine of the most important works of art and many rare books, as well as Hardwick Hall and its supporting farms and woods, were surrendered to the Treasury in lieu of cash. Thousands of acres of land and other assets were sold. The negotiations took seventeen years to complete and the final payment was made in 1967. The ownership of all the remaining Derbyshire estates then passed to the Trustees of the Chatsworth Settlement.

The 11th Duke and his family lived at Edensor House in the park from 1947. In 1957 the decision was taken to move back to Chatsworth. Some internal modernisation was done, including a new central heating system and changes of use for some of the rooms. A new kitchen was fitted up nearer the private dining room and six flats made for members of staff and their families. In November 1959 the work was completed and the family moved in. They occupy rooms on the ground and first floors, for which the Duke pays rent. While the house, garden and park were the property of the Trustees of the Chatsworth Settlement the present Duke insisted that no application for public funds towards upkeep should be made.

On 31st March 1981, after three years of negotiations with the government, the running of Chatsworth was taken over by the Chatsworth House Trust Ltd. This is a charitable foundation set up by the present Duke to help ensure for the public benefit the preservation of the house, its essential contents, the garden and the park. The Trust has been granted a 99-year lease and provided with a large permanent endowment from the family trust, produced from sales from the library and the art collection from the private side of the house. It is hoped that the annual income from this endowment, added to that from visitors to the house and garden each year, will cover the costs of maintaining Chatsworth House and its garden and park. To these visitors the Duke and his family and all the staff at Chatsworth are extremely grateful.

BEHIND THE SCENES

Beneath Chatsworth's 1.3 acres of roof, there are 175 rooms, 3,426 feet of passages, 17 staircases and 359 doors, all lit by 2,084 light bulbs. There are 397 external window frames, 62 internal window frames, 5 roof lanterns and 60 roof lights with a grand total of 7,873 panes of glass. 27 baths, 55 wash hand basins, 29 sinks, 6 wash ups and 56 lavatories complete these unusual statistics.

The paintwork and gilding of the Library being restored in 1983

The house and garden together provide around 66 full time and 23 part time jobs. Many of these people learn their trade on the estate, and most of them live in estate houses in the villages of Edensor, Pilsley, Beeley and Calton Lees. In the summer they are joined by 100 more people, many of them part time, who work as wardens, ticket sellers, shop assistants, car parkers, guides, cooks and waitresses.

The Chatsworth Fire Team

The administration of the house is the responsibility of the Comptroller and he heads the permanent maintenance staff who are needed to ensure the preservation of the building and its treasures. The work of the joiners may involve anything from shovelling snow off the roof or moving statues to making a garden paybox or restoring the China Closet; together with the electricians, plumbers, painters, a mason, seamstresses, security men, telephonists and drivers, they also have an important rôle as members of the fire and salvage teams.

Many of the rooms in the North Wing are now staff flats, offices, workshops and storerooms. The Victorian kitchen is the joiner's shop, the laundry and servants' hall are now archive stores, and the theatre is a textile conservation room.

During the winter, the Housekeeper and her staff spring clean the public route; every piece of china and the glass chandeliers are washed, the floors and furniture polished, the carvings dusted and leather books treated.

The works of art are looked after by the Keeper of the Collections, assisted by a Librarian, Archivist and Silver Steward. As well as being responsible for the condition and cataloguing of the collections, and the loan of objects to exhibitions, the Keeper of the Collections and the Comptroller supervise large scale restoration projects. Every year a considerable sum is set aside in the budget for this work, which is carried out without any public grants. Major works that have been completed recently include the cleaning of painted ceilings, the re-gilding of external window frames, the restoration of Flora's Temple and the Cascade House and the repair of woodworm damage to the limewood carvings.

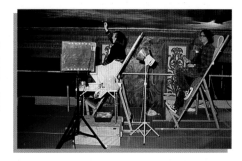

Conservators restoring the Painted Hall ceiling, January 1996

An education service is provided for schools who visit the estate. Children study a variety of subjects with the help of special publications and guided tours. Chatsworth provides surroundings in which children can broaden their knowledge and understanding of history, art, geography, science and technology.

Chatsworth has a tradition of long service. In 1963 the Duke gave a party for people who had worked on the Derbyshire estate for 25 years or longer. 175 people came, of whom 123 had done 25 years or more and 52 had completed over 40 years. Since then awards have been given at the annual staff party. By 1996 there had been 197 for 25 years and 101 for 40 years.

Preparation in the Great Dining Room for the Society of Dilettanti dinner, 1994

THE CARRIAGE HOUSE RESTAURANT AND SHOP

In 1991 a new restaurant was opened in the former Carriage House, built behind the stables by the 6th Duke in the 1840s. During the season the restaurant caters for more than 20,000 people a month and a number of private and charitable events take place in the Carriage House during the year.

The State Coach, displayed on the balcony of the Restaurant, was brought to Chatsworth in the 1890s by Duchess Louise, wife of the 8th Duke. It was used by the present Duke and Duchess and their son Lord Hartington, then aged 9, at the coronation of the Queen in 1953. Lord Hartington was page to his grandmother, Mary Duchess of Devonshire, who was Mistress of the Robes to Her Majesty.

The Carriage House shop in the old covered ride which is open to visitors from the park was also established in 1991.

FURTHER READING

Duchess of Devonshire *The House: a portrait of Chatsworth*. Macmillan, 1982. Paperback edition 1987.

Duchess of Devonshire *The Estate: a View from Chatsworth*. Macmillan, 1990. Paperback edition 1992.

Duchess of Devonshire *Farm Animals: based on the farmyard at Chatsworth* (for children). Kyle Cathie, 1991.

Duchess of Devonshire *Treasures of Chatsworth: a private view*. Constable 1991.

F. Thompson *A history of Chatsworth*. Country Life, 1949.

F. Thompson *Chatsworth: a short history*. Country Life, 1951.

J. Lees-Milne & J. Cornforth *Chatsworth: home of the Dukes of Devonshire*. (9 articles in Country Life, April-September 1968).

THE CAVENDISH FAMILY

J. Pearson *Stags and Serpents: the story of the House of Cavendish*. Macmillan 1983.

D. N. Durant *Bess of Hardwick: portrait of an Elizabethan dynast*. Weidenfeld & Nicolson, 1977.

B. Masters *Georgiana, Duchess of Devonshire*. Hamish Hamilton 1981.

J. Lees-Milne *The Bachelor Duke: William Spencer Cavendish, 6th Duke of Devonshire, 1790–1858*. John Murray, 1991.

THE CHATSWORTH ESTATE

Chatsworth is the centre of a 35,000 acre estate, encompassing farms, woods, moorland, rivers, villages, quarries and other industries both large and small. The house is surrounded by a 1,000 acre park, which is enclosed by a nine mile deer fence. People have always been welcome to walk, to bring their children and dogs, picnic and play games at any time of year.

The Farmyard is designed to be an entertaining, but non-sentimental, way of explaining the life-cycles and ultimate uses of the ordinary commercial farm stock on the estate, while the Adventure Playground delights children of all ages.

Chatsworth
Farm Shop
Tel: 01246 583392

The Farmshop, in Pilsley, set up in 1976, is now established as one of the finest food shops in the country. Focusing initially on Chatsworth produce, such as meat, game, dairy products, potatoes and flour, the shop has now expanded to sell other British foods and wines.

The woods, farms and other businesses that make up the Derbyshire estate, including as far afield as Buxton and Bolsover, are administered from the Estate Office. This is an 18th century brick building on the edge of the park, originally built as an hotel for visitors to Chatsworth, which has always been open to the public.

THE BOLTON ABBEY ESTATE
Skipton, North Yorkshire

Dipper

Red Grouse

The family trust also owns the Bolton Abbey estate in the Yorkshire Dales National Park. The ruins of the Priory, on the bank of the River Wharfe, are surrounded by some of the most beautiful country in England. Open all year, the estate provides miles of walks on the moors, in the woods and by the river.

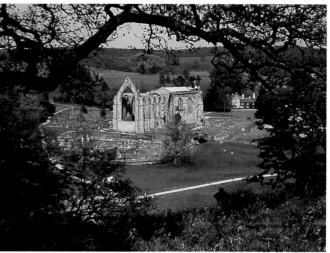

Of the many services provided for visitors to the estate the best known is the Devonshire Arms Country House Hotel, set in 12 acres of parkland, and largely fitted with furniture and paintings from Chatsworth.

Bolton Abbey Estate – Tel 01756 710533

The Devonshire Arms Country House Hotel,
Bolton Abbey, Near Skipton,
North Yorkshire BD23 6AJ
Tel 01756 710441
Fax: 01756 710564